The
REST
of the
STORY

by Mary Kathryn Johnson

Queenship

PUBLISHING COMPANY
P.O. Box 220 • Goleta, CA 93116
(800) 647-9882 • (805) 692-0043 • Fax: (805) 967-5843

To Saint Catherine Laboure of the Miraculous Medal Blessed Mother said, "All who wear it will receive great graces."

To Mary Kathryn of the Virgin of the Globe Medal Blessed Mother said, "There will be great protection for those who will wear this medal in these days of battle." Given Oct. 13, 1992.

For audio and video tapes and further information please write.

Mission Canyon
P.O. Box 67
Kirkland, AZ 86332

(Dedicated to continuing the mission of St. Catherine Laboure)

Library of Congress Number # 00-132054

Published by:
Queenship Publishing
P.O. Box 220
Goleta, CA 93116
(800) 647-9882 • (805) 692-0043 • Fax: (805) 967-5843
http://www.queenship.org

Printed in the United States of America

ISBN: 1-57918-128-7

Foreword

When Our Blessed Mother appeared to St.. Catherine Laboure in November of 1830, her second apparition had two phases. In the first phase, She appeared as the Virgin With the Golden Ball. In the second phase, She appeared as the Immaculate Conception. For whatever reason, known only to God, the second phase of the apparition received greater attention, so much so that a statue was made and a medal was struck of Mary as the Immaculate Conception, the medal which began to be called the Miraculous Medal. The first phase of the apparition was passed over for some years, but before St. Catherine went to the Lord, the statue of the Virgin With the Golden Ball was made, though incompletely because the rays coming from Mary's rings were not included, nor was the medal struck.

It would seem that heaven had made a mistake. Why was the first phase given only in part? Heaven never makes mistakes; it only pauses to permit time to pass before it completes what it has begun. In 1994, a medal of the Virgin of the first phase was struck, and on January 6th of 2001, a statue was finally made in the exact way in which Our Lady appeared. Why that passage of time? The first phase, though it had its beginning at the same time as the Medal and Statue of the Immaculate Conception, was planned and ordained for the present day so as to give emphasis and place importance on the quality of mercy.

The mission of St. Catherine Laboure was finally completed through the instrumentality of Mary Kathryn Johnson, a widow with two children, living in the United States, within the diocese of Phoenix, Arizona. Experiencing within her a strong command to follow through on Mary's wishes, she presented herself to the powers at hand at Rue du Bac. She was sent to her bishop with the task at hand, and with the assistance of her spiritual director of that time, made the appointment and was given by the bishop, his assistant chancellor, the permission to proceed in her work. That work has begun and presently flourishes. Somewhere in the elapse of time, the first phase of St. Catherine's apparition became known as the Virgin of the Globe/the Virgin Most Powerful. Our Lady has made the request that the medal finds its way around the necks of all of Her children for the purpose of receiving protection by Her in these days of the battle.

The booklet in your hand will unfold for you all the details so that you might personally find your way into this special protection and help all of your loved ones, young and old, to benefit from this very special gift given to the world in these terror-stricken days. The Virgin Most Powerful, because She is Immaculately Conceived, presents and offers Herself in our day to all of Her childern on earth as the Mediatrix, Co-redemptrix and Advocate.

Fr. Stephen Valenta, OFM Conv.
(Mary Kathryn Johnson's Spiritual Director)

The Rest of the Story

As the evening Angelus rang over Burgundy, on the second of May, 1806, the eve of the Feast of the Finding of the Holy Cross, Catherine Laboure was born to Pierre Laboure and his wife, Madeleine Louise (Gontard).

Coincidence? Catherine's biographer, Joseph I. Dirvin, C.M., reminds us, "…everything we call coincidence — is not one with God. It is part of His plan, a sign post He places along the way of a soul." Catherine was a happy child, full of goodness and piety, and she had a special relationship with her mother, from whom she learned the "beginnings of sanctity." Catherine was only nine years old when her mother died. That is a tender age for a little girl. But soon after her mother's burial, Catherine took Our Lady for her Mother.

Climbing up on a chair, she took down the family's statue of Mary, hugged it close to her, and said aloud, "Now, dear Blessed Mother, now you will be my Mother!" We might never have known this, but Heaven arranged for a servant to witness it, unnoticed by Catherine — a quiet, intensely personal moment, a solemn choice, with great and wonderful consequences throughout the world in time to come.

Catherine (called Zoe in her childhood) and her sister, Tonine, went to live with their aunt Marguerite (Laboure) Jeanrot for two years after their mother's death. Their aunt was a gentle, loving woman, and in time the two little girls found contentment, but Catherine never forgot whom she had chosen as her Mother. After this time, the girls returned home to their father's house.

It was only a few weeks later that Catherine received her First Holy Communion on January 25, 1818, the feast of the Conversion of St. Paul. It was at this time that the bud of her piety blossomed, and she began to display more and more her intense love for God and Our Lady. Father Dirvin tells us, "We can only conclude that God himself was her director...," and from this time on she talked about her vocation openly.

When Catherine was eighteen, she experienced a dream. In this dream she was told, by an old and holy priest whom she did not recognize: "...You flee from me now, but one day you will be glad to come to me. God has plans for you, do not forget it."

Almost four years later, Catherine, while visiting the Hospice de la Charite, run by the sisters of St. Vincent de Paul, saw a portrait on the wall — it was the venerable priest she had seen in her dream. It was St. Vincent de Paul himself. When she related this, and her mysterious dream, to her confessor, he said to her: "St. Vincent de Paul calls you. He wishes you to be a Sister of Charity." Reluctantly, her father finally consented, but he refused her a dowry. Catherine understood and accepted her father as he was, and she returned this act with love and compassion, and hence, Heaven removed this and all other obstacles still remaining to her vocation.

On January 22, 1830 Catherine entered the religious life at the Hospice de la Charite in Chatillon-sur-Seine, her dowry and trousseau supplied by her brother Hubert Laboure and his wife Jeanne.

Catherine was little known by the members of St. Vincent de Paul's "two families," the Sisters of Charity and the Vincentian Fathers, but well known by St. Vincent. In time she shared with him all that was in her heart, and he shared with her his heart, literally. His heart appeared to her on three consecutive evenings, each night a different color, denoting different meanings. On the third night Catherine heard for the first time an interior voice: **"The heart of St. Vincent is deeply afflicted at the sorrows that will befall France."** These apparitions of the heart of St. Vincent were repeated eight or nine times. Catherine's life would never be the same, as is true with all whom God chooses to receive such graces. It may seem to some that this would mean great joy, and in truth it does, but not without great sufferings as well. They are intertwined like branches from the One True Vine.

These visions of the Heart of St. Vincent de Paul were not the only visions Catherine was to experience. As a postulant, she frequently beheld Our Lord visible in the Blessed Sacrament during Mass.

It was on July 18, 1830, that Catherine's First Apparition took place. It is commonly called the "Virgin of the Chair." It was the eve of the feast of St. Vincent de Paul. Catherine was awakened by an angel, who appeared as a small child, and escorted her to the chapel where she first saw the Blessed Mother. She had asked for this since she was a small child. (St. Therese of the Child Jesus and the Holy Face tells us that the Lord often made her desire what He wanted to give her. We can assume then, that this was also the case with Catherine.)

In this first apparition, Our Lady was seated and Catherine, at Her knee, rested her hands upon Her lap, and they talked for over two hours. They talked of God's plans, for Catherine, for her Community, for France, and the whole world. Our Lady said to her, **"My child, the good God wishes to charge you with a mission."**

The child accompanied Catherine back to the dormitory after the apparition and then faded from sight as Our Lady had. Catherine felt certain that he was her guardian angel.

Catherine's second apparition is commonly referred to as "The Great Apparition of November 27," 1830, however, the one apparition of that date was given two numbers, #2 and #3, to designate the two phases of the Medal shown to Catherine. Therein lies the confusion. Some people have come to refer to the "three" Apparitions of St. Catherine Laboure, when, in fact there were only two — *the second having two phases.*

The second apparition, then, took place as the sisters were gathered for their evening meditation. Suddenly Catherine was enveloped in a great stillness, and in her heart she knew what was coming.

The First Phase: There, in the sanctuary, standing upon a globe, was the Virgin Mary, Queen of Heaven, visible only to Catherine. Our Lady held in Her hands a golden ball which She offered to God, with Her eyes raised toward Heaven, and from the stones in the rings on her fingers, brilliant light shown down upon the globe at Her feet. Then She looked down at Sister Laboure and She said, **"The ball which you see represents the whole world,**

especially **France, and each person in particular. These rays symbolize the graces I shed upon those who ask for them. The gems from which rays do not fall are the graces for which souls forget to ask."**

The Second Phase: Then the golden ball disappeared and Mary's arms swung wide, the rays of light still streaming from the jewels on Her fingers, the symbol of a great outpouring of graces. There was an oval frame of words around the Blessed Virgin which read, **"O Mary, conceived without sin, pray for us who have recourse to thee."**

And Our Lady said, **"Have a Medal struck after this model. All who wear it will receive great graces, they should wear it around the neck. Graces will abound for persons who wear it with confidence."**

Our Lady showed St. Catherine the Medal She desired in two "phases." Why, if there was no need?

Should we wonder then, why the Medal would be produced in *two phases?* There would be a "time" for each. One does not take away from the other. It is not possible for Our Lady to be in competition with Herself.

Then Catherine was shown the reverse side of the Medal, which contained a large M surmounted by a bar and a cross. Beneath were the Hearts of Jesus, crowned with thorns, and Mary, pierced with a sword. Twelve stars encircled the whole. The back of the Medal was shown to Catherine only once, as it would remain unchanged.

In his definitive biography of St. Catherine Laboure, Father Dirvin tells us that the Medal design submitted and subsequently engraved in 1832 was not the *phase* of the Apparition of November 27 that was originally intended, which was "The Virgin of the Globe," also called "The Virgin Most Powerful."

He says, "Father Chevalier, Catherine's last director, in his deposition before the Beatification Tribunal, expressed the opinion that the change was made because of the difficulty of representing the attitude of the first *phase* in metal, and also because Father Aladel, Catherine's confessor, thought it more prudent, in view of the anti-religious feeling at the time, to represent Our Lady in the attitude of "…what he called the second *phase*."

In light of the events of the present day, concerning Pope John Paul II's desire to proclaim the 5th Marian Dogma, and the bringing forth of the Virgin of the Globe Medal at this time, Father Aladel's concerns can be seen in the light of truth, then and now.

But Heaven does not make mistakes; the first *phase* was to be last and the last was to be first. And so Catherine and Heaven accepted the first Medal, which was called the Medal of the Immaculate Conception, although it *preceded* the Dogma of the Immaculate Conception. It came to be called the Miraculous Medal by the people because of the many wonders reported in connection with it.

Catherine has often been called the Saint of Silence because for forty-six years she kept the secret that she was indeed the Seer. Pope Pius XI said at the Beatification ceremonies in 1933, "To think of keeping a secret for forty-six years, and this by a woman, and a Sister!"

During these years, Catherine was tormented that the statue of the Virgin of the Globe, for which Our Lady had asked, had not been made. In 1876, Catherine was sure that she would not live much longer, and she asked the Blessed Virgin's permission to speak. Having received it, Catherine told the whole story of her visions to Sister Dufes, her Superior, *and she stressed that the statue must be made!* The statue of Our Lady holding the golden ball and offering it to God!

These are the words taken from her autobiography.

"Sister Dufes was completely bewildered. 'But I have never heard tell of this detail,' she cried, 'If you speak of such an attitude now, they will say you have grown foolish!'"

"It will not be the first time they have said that of me," Catherine replied, *"but until the moment I die, I shall insist that the Blessed Virgin appeared to me holding a ball in her hands."*

"What became of the ball?" Sister Dufes asked.

"Oh, I do not know, I only know that suddenly I saw rays falling upon the globe on which Our Lady stood, and especially upon a spot where 'France' was written."

"How about the Medal? Is it necessary to change the design?"

"Do not touch the Medal," Catherine replied. **"It is only nec-**

essary to erect an altar on the spot of the Apparition, as the Blessed Virgin asked, and to place above it her statue, with a ball in her hands."

Sister Dufes was still doubtful. "They are not going to believe you," she persisted. "Is there anyone who can confirm your story?

"Yes," Catherine said, considering, "yes, there is someone. Sister Grand, who was secretary in the Mother house at the time, and who took notes of the Apparition from Father Aladel's dictation."

Sister Dufes wrote at once to Sister Grand. Sister Grand replied that all Catherine had said was true. She even included some rough sketches of the proposed statue which had been drawn at the time.

Shortly before her death, Catherine saw the finished plaster model from which the statue would be carved. "Her disappointment was keen." (St. Catherine Laboure of The Miraculous Medal).

In her final illness Catherine was asked whether she was afraid to die, and she answered, "Why should I be afraid. I am going to see Our Lord and the Blessed Virgin and St. Vincent."

At seven o'clock on the 31st of December 1876 Sister Catherine Laboure was born into eternal life.

Her incorrupt body was disinterred in 1933 following the announcement of her beatification. It lies, still, in the side altar, behind covered glass in the chapel at Rue du Bac, beneath the statue of the Virgin of the Globe, exactly where Our Lady Herself had requested that the statue be put — that is, where Our Lady actually appeared to her, showing her the *two phases* of the Medal. And nearby, in a beautiful reliquary, the incorrupt heart of St. Vincent de Paul.

St. Catherine was *canonized* on July 27, 1947.

But her story does not end there. From Heaven her mission continues.

For those of you who would like to know more about St Catherine Laboure, we refer you to the book, *Saint Catherine Laboure of the Miraculous Medal*, a definitive biography by Joseph I. Dirvin, C.M.

On December 11, 1945, the eve of the feast of Our Lady of Guadalupe (Mother of the America's), a baby girl was born to Thomas Robert Madera and his wife, Loretta Ann (Purington). All during her mother's pregnancy it was said that, if the child was a girl, her name would be Rita Renee, but Heaven had other plans. Just a few days before her birth, the doctor said this child would surely be born on December 8th, the Feast of the Immaculate Conception, (one day, Our Lady would refer to this as the day of her "anticipation"), and so, at her Grandmother Purington's insistence, it was decided that, if it was a girl, her name *must* be Mary! And to go with the name Mary, Kathryn was chosen. Her parents gave no thought to this second name in terms of a particular saint. (This is interesting, in light of the fact that Blessed Catherine Laboure was not canonized until 1947, though as certainly in heaven, she already was a saint.)

She was born during the 8 p.m. hour in Mercy Hospital, Des Moines, Iowa, United States of America.

She was baptized on the 27th of January 1946, at Saint Ambrose Cathedral, Des Moines, Iowa. Besides the Priest who baptized her, there was also a Monsignor present who took off the medal of Our Lady from around his neck and placed it around the neck of the infant. Her mother related this story to her as she grew older.

The medal, on a little blue ribbon, was placed by her mother in her baby book. (It was traditional at that time that the Miraculous Medal was worn around the neck of the children with a blue ribbon). As a young child, Mary Kathryn wanted so much to wear the medal of Our Lady. One day she took it from her baby book and wore it to school without her mother's permission and lost it. She would not remember, in years to come, if indeed this had been the Miraculous Medal, because she had never heard the story of the Miraculous Medal. Nor had she been shown one. But her sorrow was great at having taken the medal without permission and lost it.

She was a sickly child. When she was grown, her mother would speak of the severe pain she had with her rheumatic fever, for which many times she had to be rushed to the hospital, but Mary Kathryn had no memory of this, nor of most of her childhood up to the age of ten, when her rheumatic fever disappeared.

One memory alone remained vivid, that of the peace and joy

she experienced at the Shrine of Mother Cabrini. Her parents took her there often during the time they lived in Colorado.

And one memory she would always "wish" she could remember, that of her First Holy Communion. She felt sure in her heart that it must have been wonderful, but for whatever reason, that memory would remain lost with the others.

Her parents took her to Holy Mass every Sunday and they prayed the family Rosary each evening, but aside from this, Mary Kathryn grew up quite ignorant of her faith. When she was in seventh grade she begged to attend Catholic School, which she did for two years. It was during this time that she felt strongly drawn to religious life, but everyone said she was "too young" and her desire was not taken seriously. It was also during this time that she was introduced to St. Therese, the Little Flower, for whom she felt a great affection, but about whom she really knew very little.

She was Confirmed on the 31st of May 1959, the Feast of the Visitation of the Blessed Virgin Mary.

She was not always good, not always pure, and not always pious, though she would always wish she had been. And she carried with her the scars of having been molested as a child. But her story was one of God's great love and mercy.

She married a young Marine, whom she loved dearly, but in 1969 he was killed in action. At the age of 23, she was a widow with two small children.

The agony of her husband's death left a great hole in her life and in her heart. Her mother said to her, "Now you must devote your life to your children and the Church!" She spoke these words with great authority. Had God shown her a glimpse of what was to be in her daughter's future?

As time passed, she longed to fill the void in her life, in a human sense, and she looked for love — in all the wrong places. In her guilt, as if to hide from God, she stepped away from the Church and the Sacraments.

Then one day she literally fell to her knees and begged God's forgiveness, saying to Him, "Lord, I have made such a mess of my life. *Please,* You take it and do with it what You will!"

In 1981, feeling the need to progress further in her spiritual walk, and not knowing how to do this, she asked the Holy Spirit to be her "Teacher," and He honored her request.

Impatient, frustrated, and new at all of this, one day she said to the Lord, "It would be so much easier if You would just give it to me in black and white!" In a short time, she began to realize that He was doing just that: Things from Scripture and other spiritual readings were "quickened" to her, as if they had been highlighted just for her.

In 1986, the Lord spoke to her interiorly for the first time. She began to write things down at that time, for fear she would forget them. She had never heard the term Prayer Journal, but that is in fact what she had been led to. She told no one. She didn't know how she could begin to explain these wonderful things that were happening to her. And besides, not knowing anyone else who had experienced such things, she felt sure people would think she was crazy.

In 1990, Our Lady spoke to her interiorly for the first time. Heaven was preparing her for something, although she did not realize it at the time.

While on pilgrimage to Medjugorje, she was given to understand that she must seek a Priest-Spiritual Director, although she did not understand the need, because she felt only "holy people" needed a spiritual director. And she did not see herself as such. Nevertheless, she followed the instructions given her to find this particular Priest, and looked for the "sign of the Holy Spirit" that she had been promised she would be given when she did. In the year that followed, she would come to feel, more and more, that *need.* And finally she whined to Our Lady, *"How long must I wait?"* Shortly after that, on Pentecost Sunday 1991, she was given the sign, and Our Lady said, **"Your search has ended."**

She approached this Priest, who was the Pastor of a large church, and explained how she had come to him. And also, that the Lord and Our Lady did speak to her internally. And she asked him if he would be her Spiritual Director. He did not know her prior to this except by sight. He told her that he had never been a Spiritual Director before. *"I've never had one before,"* she said.

"Then," he said, "we'll let the Holy Spirit guide us." He accepted her without hesitation, though she would be told later, by people who had known this priest for years, that he "Never says 'yes' to anything! His first answer is always 'no,' and then after he's had time to think about it, he may or may not come back and say 'yes.'"

It was on September 10, 1991 that she first heard the voice of Saint Catherine internally. She said, **"Your day begins with prayer and it ends with prayer, and everything in between is prayer. Your whole life becomes a prayer when offered to God. In all that you say and do, remember this."**

Mary Kathryn asked who was speaking, and the gentle voice answered, **"A guide; a friend."**

"May I ask your name?"

"I am Catherine."

"Are you a Catherine I should know?"

"You will know me," was the reply.

On September 29, 1991, Mary Kathryn was thanking the Lord, and those whom He had allowed her to speak with. And she said, "And thank you, Catherine, whoever you are."

It was then she heard **"Laboure."** She did not know who Catherine Laboure was, but thinking that she might be a saint, she went to her little book of Saints and there she was. Along with the story, in brief, of the Miraculous Medal. This was the first time she could remember having ever heard of it.

She asked Catherine if she was her Patron Saint. Catherine said that indeed she was. **"...I have known you even when you did not know me, but,"** she said, **"there are other reasons for this kind of introduction and developing relationship...."** She did not say what those reasons were. Only that she would come to assist her, when there was need.

Mary Kathryn shared with a friend the wonderful discovery that Catherine Laboure was her Patron Saint. But she knew almost nothing about her.

Her friend sent her a book, *St. Catherine Laboure of the Miraculous Medal.* On May 16, 1992, as she turned to page 96, she had an intense interior experience. And in a moment of time, she understood that the Blessed Mother wanted the other *phase:* the "other Medal" struck now!

And Catherine said to her, **"Go to your Spiritual Director, as I went to mine. He will assist you."**

In shock, she replied, "Me? How can I?"

And again Catherine repeated, **"He will assist you."**

She did not have the opportunity to speak with her Spiritual Director and tell him what had happened until May 31st, the feast of the Visitation of the Blessed Virgin Mary.

In the meantime, on May 27, Our Lady said to her, **"I want you to come to Fatima."** Mary Kathryn saw no connection with the Medal, and no way financially for this to happen, but she said to Our Lady, *"…if You desire it to be so, I believe it will. I don't understand why, but I don't have to."*

There on the table in front of her lay the *Soul* magazine. She opened it, and this is what she read: "Fatima, absorbed in that quiet listening to God which characterizes her, continues to be a constant point of reference and of appeal to live the Gospel . . . From the Cova da Iria a comforting light seems to spread, full of hope which gives light to the facts that characterize the end of this millennium.…" (Pope John Paul II).

When she met with her Spiritual Director, she told him what she had experienced and related to him Our Lady's desire concerning the Medal. He instructed her to wait and pray for more direction. It was also on this night he informed her that he was to be transferred out of state in a few months. As they parted that evening, he said to her, "Never be afraid to share what the Lord has given you."

She waited and she prayed.…

On June 8th, 1992, not having received anything further concerning the Medal, she said to the Blessed Mother, "…I pray, as my Spiritual Director has directed me, that You will make it more clear to me about the Medal." And the Blessed Mother said, **"I shall."** But she didn't say when.

On June 9th, Mary Kathryn inquired of a friend, if by chance she would be taking any pilgrimages to Fatima, and she said that there was one planned for November. It would also include Lourdes and at the request of the Priest-Spiritual Director for the pilgrimage, Paris had been added to the itinerary in order to allow for a visit to Rue du Bac, the Shrine of the Miraculous Medal.

Mary Kathryn had been introduced to this priest on a previous pilgrimage to Medjugorje and she felt very drawn to him spiritually, although he was unaware of that.

He really knew nothing about her except her name and where she lived.

Her current Spiritual Director was to be reassigned in January 1993. And so, Mary Kathryn spoke with him about the possibility of asking the other priest to be her Spiritual Director when this would happen. He instructed her to speak with the other priest and ask if he would accept her. She did so on September 4, 1992.

On that morning, before her appointment with him, she said, *"Lead me where You will, Blessed Mother — and where **He wills**. Is this the one?"*

She was immediately lead to the following Scripture:

> Come to me, all you that need instruction, and learn in my school.... Here is what I say. [and here the Lord interjected, '**to you**'] It costs nothing to be wise. Put on the yoke, and be willing to learn. The opportunity is always near ... no matter how much it costs you to get Wisdom, it will be worth it. Be joyfully grateful for the Lord's mercy, and never be ashamed to praise Him. Do your duty at the proper time, and the Lord, at the time he thinks proper, will give you your reward. (Sirach 51:23, 25, 26, 28-30)

She did not understand what this had to do with whether or not the other priest was to be her Spiritual Director. And so the Lord said to her, **"Ask the priest to explain it to you. Therein you shall have your answer."**

Later that day she met with the other priest. When she shared with him the Scripture from Sirach, he explained to her that this was the "call of a rabbi to a student to come and be taught," and he said, that if indeed the Lord was calling her to him, that he was to teach her "basics." "That is what I do. I teach," he said. She was very happy to hear that, because there was so much she did not know and she was hungry to learn.

Among other things, she shared with him Our Lady's desire concerning the Medal. He said that he would pray and discern until after the pilgrimage. Then, he would give her his answer as to whether or not he would be her Spiritual Director. But in regards to the Medal, he said he felt that it should be presented at Rue du Bac. And she must do it alone with only an interpreter. He told her to "go with no expectations of what will happen there!"

When she met next with her current Spiritual Director, she reported to him what had happened in her meeting with the other priest. He agreed with everything that had been told to her by him.

On October 1ˢᵗ, St. Catherine said to her, **"The time approaches as surely as the passage of time in all things is a part of God's plan."**

October 9ᵗʰ, St. Catherine said, **". . . the passage of time was necessary. You were born with the capacities required for the mission which God intends to intrust to you, as was I. You have only to proceed without fear."**

On October 12ᵗʰ, while reading *The Last Days of Maximilian Kolbe,* which had been assigned to her to read before the pilgrimage by the other priest who was considering her as a directee, Mary Kathryn wrote in her journal these quotes:

Love ... would enable him to keep every promise.

...the will of the Immaculate always manifests itself through obedience.

Militia Immaculatae — to the skeptical, knowing eyes of a worldling, it might even seem absurd. A prayer and a medal — to bring about the conversion, even the sanctification, of half of humanity!

(The Last Days of Maximilian Kolbe)

And she asked, "Do you want a prayer, too, my Lady?"

"The prayer is the same. The Medal is the same as that for which I asked. Only the time is different."

> ...time has shown that the disbelieving know-it-all eyes of the world simply cannot grasp certain aspects of reality.
>
> *(The Last Days of Maximilian Kolbe)*

On October 13th, while praying in the little chapel in her home, she prayed in thanksgiving for the protection she had recently received during a pronounced attack by the evil one. Our Lady appeared to her interiorly as the Virgin of the Globe. She had not seen Her as such before, and so she asked if there was a significance to seeing Her in this way at this particular time. Our Lady said, **"Yes, *there will be Great Protection for those who will wear this medal in these days of battle.* Satan is aware of this, as he is aware of you, but do not fear. I am with you always. More will be revealed to you. Come, my little one."** [She understood this to mean "come to Fatima."]

On October 23, she saw Her again, interiorly, as the Virgin of the Globe, only this time she was standing in the middle of a beautiful fountain: the water sprayed up from her feet and out at her shoulders. She said, **"Did you bring your buckets, my children?"** Mary Kathryn recalled that the Lord had told Blessed Faustina that the bucket with which one draws from the fount of Mercy is trust.

These were the only two times Our Lady showed herself to Mary Kathryn as the Virgin of the Globe/The Virgin Most Powerful.

All of Mary Kathryn's visions were internal, not external, and they happened infrequently, as opposed to the frequent interior conversations which took place at this time.

On October 31st, All Hallow's Eve, the night before the pilgrimage, the Lord said to her, **"What My Mother asks, I ask. Follow Her and you are within My Will."**

The day of the pilgrimage arrived, November 1, 1992, All Saints Day. The next day, November 2, All Souls Day, they were in Fatima where Mary Kathryn experienced much interiorly, for which she says she has no words, except to say that, "What happened at Fatima not only was, but is."

A priest there, during her confession, whom she did not know, said to her, "You are one of those prime individuals called by the Sacred Heart of Jesus and the Immaculate Heart of Mary. You have something they want . . ."

As the pilgrimage departed for France, Our Lady said, **"Prepare yourself for many trials. Pray many Rosaries. Each will be a link in your armor ... pray much for those who kill the innocents. If they do not beg God's forgiveness in this life, they will surely burn in hell.**

"Pray daily for the Baptism of the tiny souls who go to meet God prematurely. The Waters of their Baptism are my tears which are many. The gravity of this horrible sin shall reach every corner of the earth. The saving Blood shall be that of the Lamb of God, and that alone. You have been given two drops to spend in reparation. Pray, Pray, Pray. Beg God for His Mercy, and console Him in His sorrow."

And at the grotto, in Lourdes, She said, **"The way is being prepared for you. Ask the intercession of those God has sent to guide you."**

At the Stations of the Cross, She said, **"...Keep the Passion of my Son ever before you."**

On the night they arrived in Paris, Mary Kathryn prayed:

> "Blessed Mother, I pray for the fulfillment of Your intentions and God's Will regarding the medal. I pray for those who will receive this message and those who will act upon it. I pray for direction and discernment in whatever You would have me do or say. Move me out of the way and let the Holy Spirit guide my actions and my words. In Jesus' Name, I ask.
>
> "Blessed Mother, please, I ask for the graces necessary to carry out what you have asked of me."

Our Lady replied, **"My child, do not fear. All is well. I shall** be with you, and those to whom you speak shall discern my presence. Look to Catherine. She will assist you."

At that, St. Catherine said, "I will assist you. Bring the Mother Superior a rose . . . She will understand."

The next morning on the way to Rue du Bac, she bought a pink rose and took it with her.

As Heaven would have it, when the time came to speak, Mary Kathryn was accompanied not by the person who she thought would be her interpreter, but by two other interpreters, a French-speaking Vietnamese priest, and a Frenchman, now living in the United States, and two personal friends — all pilgrims.

Mary Kathryn thought surely she would be speaking to the Mother Superior, and so when they arrived at the reception area, she asked if she might do so. The nun behind the desk insisted she had to know why. Mary Kathryn simply said, "I have a message for her." The nun insisted she must know who the message was from. When the answer was given, "Mary," she stepped away and brought another nun out to talk to her. This stern-looking nun informed her, rather curtly, that the Mother Superior was "out of the country!" When she asked if she might speak with whoever was next in charge, she was told that she also was "out of the country!"

Impatiently the gentleman friend with her asked, "Isn't there anyone in charge here?"

Mary Kathryn, a little concerned about what he might say next, asked if she might speak with a priest, and was told that she could.

Her friends waited outside while she went into a small room with the interpreters. It had to be this way to fulfill the priest's instructions that she must do this alone — with only her interpreters.

The priest she was presented to was sitting behind a small desk and his body language and facial expression were guarded at best. She asked if she might ask his name, but he chose not to give it. He did say that he was only there on temporary assignment.

"Although he looked at me like I was a little crazy, I watched his eyes as we spoke, and they seemed to become softer and softer, and finally he even smiled."

He said to her, through the interpreters, "If the Blessed Mother Herself were standing right next to you, we could not help you here because Rue du Bac is not a parish." He said she must begin at the parish level (in her own parish) and go through the Bishop of her diocese, and that if what she was saying was true she had nothing to fear. She told him she was not afraid, (precisely for that reason).

"Although, I was a little nervous," she admits.

Shortly after that, he got up and left the room. She asked the interpreters where he was going. They told her that he had gone to find her a relic of St. Catherine, but he returned empty handed. There were none to be found, he said.

She thanked him and asked him if he would please pray for Our Lady's intentions. He said that he would.

As she stepped outside, suddenly she felt great joy in her heart, with a knowing that it was Our Lady who was actually the Mother Superior of that place!

She went into the Chapel with her friends and knelt in front of the incorrupt body of St. Catherine, with the statue of the Virgin of the Globe above it. A nun was walking up onto the main altar just to her left. As she passed, Mary Kathryn reached out, smiled, and handed her the rose and pointed to the statue of Our Lady on the altar (assuming she did not speak English). The nun smiled back and took the rose. She had understood this wordless request. She knew for whom the rose was intended.

There was something in the right hand of the statue of Our Lady on the main altar, but Mary Kathryn couldn't make out what it was. Later she would learn that it was a key, and the priest had asked (because it was very meaningful to him), why the key was in her hand. He was told that it was because She is the Head of the house, and so She holds the key. Confirmation that, indeed, She was the Mother Superior there.

At the foot of the Altar, Our Lady said to her, **"It is good that you have come. The graces you receive here will give you strength and courage for what is to come."**

St. Catherine said, **"You will have much to suffer, but God's love will sustain you."**

Following the celebration of the Holy Mass there, the Blessed Mother asked, **"My child, what have you learned here?** *"Obedience and humility"* Mary Kathryn answered. Our Lady added, **"And perseverance. Do not expect a paved road, but walk on … Pray many Rosaries."**

On the return to the United States, Mary Kathryn met with the other priest who had been considering her. He agreed with the priest from Rue du Bac concerning the medal. He also agreed to be her Spiritual Director — when her current Spiritual Director was transferred.

She met with the priest who was still her Spiritual Director and he agreed that this was the proper way to proceed in regard to both her Spiritual Direction and the Medal.

On Novermber 17ᵗʰ, Our Lady said to Mary Kathryn, **"I am the Immaculate Conception. I am Full of Grace. The world has forgotten. It needs to be reminded. Those who turn to me will receive the graces which flow from my hands. Let them know they do have recourse to me."**

Later, feeling prompted to do so, she looked up this word: *Recourse* — access or resort to a person or thing for help or *protection. (The Random House Dictionary of the English Language).*

"Proceed. In God's time all will come to pass." Our Lady said.

Mary Kathryn asked, *"Blessed Mother, why were these things not given to me on the pilgrimage?"* (It seemed to her, in her humanness, that this would have been a good place and time for such teachings.)

And Our Lady replied, **"What was given to you was proper and prudent for the time."**

Again she felt called to look this word up in the dictionary, although she felt sure she already understood its meaning. *Prudent* — careful in providing for the future … *provident. (The Random House Dictionary of the English Language)*

Mary Kathryn's parish priest was also her confessor. The Lord had specifically requested that he be. However, she had not spoken to him in regard to the Medal, since he was not her Spiritual Director, and there didn't seem to be a need until now. All three priests, her first Spiritual Director, her second Spiritual Director and her parish priest/confessor, were from different parishes within the same diocese.

Her parish priest/confessor was very conservative and Mary Kathryn was not at all sure of how he would react to this news. Much to her surprise, he was more than receptive and said he would have "no problem" presenting her to the Bishop. And he took a book from his shelf and shared with her this quotation from Elizabeth Ann Seton:

> "I will tell you what is my own great help. I once read or heard that the interior life means but the continuation of our Savior's life in us; that the great object of all His mysteries is to merit for us the grace of His interior life and communicate it to us, it being the end of His mission to lead us into the sweet land of promise, a life of constant union with Himself. And what was the first rule of our dear Savior's life? You know it was to do His Father's Will. Well, then, the first end I propose in our daily work is to *do the Will of God,* secondly, to *do it in the manner He Wills and to do it because He Wills....*"

He wrote to the Bishop, but told Mary Kathryn that it could take a long time for an answer because the Bishop was so busy. However, the reply was not long at all in coming. The priest called her into his office when he received the response and told her that the Bishop was wondering why he had not yet heard from her. So he instructed her to write to him.

He also told her that he had been instucted not to encourage her. Then he put his hand on her shoulder and said, "But don't give up the ship!" ("I feel sure he would not mind me telling this now. He died just after the first gold medal was minted.")

On February 17, 1993, Mary Kathryn wrote to the Bishop and told him about Our Lady's request for the Medal and requested to speak with him. She also assured him that she would be obedient to his direction, whatever that might be.

In response, inquiries were made by the Assistant Chancellor, after which she received a letter from him dated March 8, 1993, telling her that the Bishop had read her letter, and reading, in part, "The Bishop has instructed me to be available should you wish to talk more about what you feel called to do."

On March 9th, Mary Kathryn told Our Lady, "Father says I need to ask You for more information about the medal. I'm not exactly sure what to ask for, but I trust You will give me what is necessary."

And She replied, *"You see, my child, that neither the medal nor the statue are complete....* **The medal protrays that I am 'Full of Grace.' The statue protrays that the world has 'recourse' to me. But to be complete, the two must be as one. Now is the time of fullness. The world must be reminded of these truths, for now is the time of the serpent and those who have confidence in me will fall under the protection of my mantle in these days of battle."**

(At another time, Our Lady told Mary Kathryn that what we wear around our necks shows what we have confidence in. She said that we need to have confidence in God and in her intercession.)

"It is pleasing to You then, that the Medal should be called the 'Completed Medal of the Immaculate Conception.'" (As Father had suggested at that time.)

"It is pleasing to God, for it was He Who conceived it so in the fullness of time."

Then there was silence and Mary Kathryn asked, "Is this all you wish to tell me, Blessed Mother?"

"For now it is enough," She said.

"St. Catherine, please pray for all those who will in any way be a part of fulfilling Our Lady's request."

And St. Catherine said, **"You will see the fulfillment of my mission, Mary Kathryn. It is your mission as well. To Jesus through Mary, our common bond. The completion of this medal shall save many souls for it will bring to fullness the portrait of the Mother of Mercy, Mediatrix of all Graces, and many will recognize Her as such who otherwise would not have known Her. And those who have forgotten to ask for graces will be reminded and blessed by her intercession. And the angels in**

Heaven shall rejoice.

"Yes, I will pray for you and for all who assist you, for in assisting you they assist Her, and in assisting Her, they assist God. The Divine plan is His. We are all but servants. Serve well, my little friend...."

On March 16, 1993, before her meeting with the Assistant Chancellor, in prayer, Mary Kathryn asked the Blessed Mother, *"Please tell me, is there anything else I should know before I meet with this priest?"*

And Our Lady said, **"My child, you have been sufficiently prepared. You have nothing to fear. The truth is all you need and you have that. Go in the grace of God."**

She was then led to this Scripture:

> There is an appointed time for everything, and a time for every affair under the heavens. A time to be born, and a time to die; a time to plant, and a time to uproot the plant. A time to kill and a time to heal; a time to tear down, and a time to build. A time to weep and a time to laugh; a time to mourn, and a time to dance. A time to scatter stones, and a time to gather them; a time to embrace and a time to be far from embraces. A time to seek, and a time to lose; a time to keep, and a time to cast away. A time to rend, and a time to sew; a time to be silent, and a time to speak. A time to love, and a time to hate; a time of war, and a time of peace.
>
> What advantage has the worker from his toil? I have considered the task which God has appointed for men to be busied about. He has made everything appropriate to its time, and has put the timeless into their hearts, without men's ever discovering, from beginning to end, the work which God has done. I recognized that there is nothing better than to be glad and to do well during life. For every man, moreover, to eat and drink and enjoy the fruit of all his labor is a gift of God. I recognized that whatever God does will endure

forever; there is no adding to it, or taking from it. Thus
has God done, that he may be revered. What now is
has already been; what is to be, already is; and God
restores what would otherwise be displaced.
(Ecclesiastes 3:1-15)

Her meeting with the Assistant Chancellor was brief and pleas-
ant. When she entered his office he asked, "How can we assist
you?" She felt that Our Lady had indeed touched his heart, and the
heart of the Bishop even prior to this meeting.

She was given "permission to proceed with what you feel called
to do," as long as she understood that the Church could not give
"approval" as it can neither prove nor disprove her experiences.

It must be noted, however, that St. Catherine Laboure's visions
and experiences have been approved by the church.

She told him that, now that she had received permission to
proceed, she hadn't the slightest idea how, but that she was not
concerned, because it was not she who was in charge.

Immediately doors were opened, and all that was needed in
expertise and finances was supplied, with little or no effort.

On March 18, 1993, in her journal she wrote, "*Father, it is
painful to do other things that must be done when all I want is to be
with You; to work for You.*"

She would not have long to wait before God would provide the
circumstances which would allow her to work for Him full-time,
though it would not be in any way as she might have pictured it.

Her journal entry dated March 25, 1993, the Feast of the Annunciation, "Many times God's Will that He sets before us will not
be the most comfortable in our lives, but He will give us courage
and strength." (Father Paco, EWTN)

In the days and weeks that followed, still begging God to let
her work for Him full-time, she began to notice greater and greater
fatigue, difficulty concentrating, memory problems and joint and
muscle pain, but she tried not to dwell on it and pressed on in her
daily activities to the best of her ability.

On April 5, 1993, Our Lady spoke of **"spiritual warfare"** and
Satan's attack **"upon the Church, the people of God."** She said,

"See how the instruments of war have changed through the centuries. See how each change with the times, became more powerful. See that which is most powerful in this time and use it."

This much was given within the context of certain lessons which Our Lady had been giving weekly for a time. Our Lady had said that these lessons were to be "shared," though Mary Kathryn did not understand how, at that time, beyond the little prayer group she belonged to, and personal friends, who in turn would share them with their friends.

Each of these "lessons" which somehow seemed connected to, yet set apart from, everything else she had received, were reviewed by the Pastor of the parish where this prayer group met, and when he was transferred, they continued to be reviewed by the new Pastor, to be sure there was nothing in them that was contrary to the teachings of the Church, faith, or morals. This continued even after Mary Kathryn became too ill to continue attending this little prayer group.

Then, personally to Mary Kathryn, Our Lady said, **"You have asked, my child, why the golden ball around my neck?"** (as she had seen on the statues at Fatima). **"This is my shield. It symbolizes the prayers of those consecrated to my Immaculate Heart, in whom I have great confidence. In Fatima I called for consecration to My Immaculate Heart of countries, yes, but moreover, of each individual. When you present yourselves to me in this way, I present you before the throne of God."**

"To Jesus through Mary."

"Yes, my little one, and when you are presented so to the King of kings, you become by His authority, Knights of the Immaculata, and your power to serve is increased."

"My Lady, You spoke of using 'that which is most powerful in this time.' I know what You are speaking of — the Medal and the Chaplet of Divine Mercy — but why didn't you mention them by name so the world would know?"

(Previously, she had been told that the Chaplet of Divine Mercy is the most powerful because in praying it, we pray in the **"perfect Will of the Father."**)

Our Lady replied, **"You will tell them for me. Did not Catherine do the same?"**

"Actually, wasn't she most powerful in her silence?"

"No," Our Lady answered, **"She was most powerful when she spoke forth my request to those who could assist her in it. You must do the same.**

"When God has wished a certain thing to be accomplished, has He not chosen His servants to accomplish it for Him throughout the ages? Has He not chosen many times the weak and the lowly and those the world would see as unsuited, that the Glory might be His?"

On April 9, 1993, Good Friday, Mary Kathryn began the Novena of Divine Mercy, as Our Lord had requested of her. This was a powerful spiritual experience for her.

On April 18th, 1993, the Feast of Divine Mercy, and the day on which Sister Faustina was Beatified, Mary Kathryn was in Stockbridge, Mass. at the Shrine of Divine Mercy. There, in an intense spiritual experience, Jesus took her into His Heart, and told her, **"When you stand before men, know that this is where you will be. Look upon them as from My Heart."**

Sister Faustina had become a special friend to her long before this.

Once, she was asked by her second Spiritual Director to sum up the whole matter of the Medal, and to his surprise, she replied, *"Mercy! — It is God's great Mercy.... That's why He sent Her."* (Divine Mercy)

It was in May 1993 that Mary Kathryn was diagnosed with Chronic Epstein Barr, a blood disorder for which there is no cure. That is what had been causing her symptoms, which by this time were greatly increased in severity, and were now constant, making it difficult for her to continue her job as office nurse for a neurologist, *"But,"* she thought, *"If I give up all other activity and just work and sleep, at least I can continue to pay my bills that way, and I can survive this."* And so she continued to press on, but each passing day was more and more difficult. The simplest task became a heavy burden!

On May 31, 1993, the Feast of the Visitation, she was led to this Scripture:

…Everything on earth honors truth; heaven praises it; all creation trembles in awe before it.

There is not the slightest injustice in truth. You will find injustice in wine, the emperor, women, all human beings, in all they do, and in everything else. There is no truth in them; they are unjust and they will perish. But truth endures and is always strong; it will continue to live and reign forever. Truth shows no partiality or favoritism; it does what is right, rather than what is unjust or evil. Everyone approves what truth does; its decisions are always fair. Truth is strong. Let all things praise the God of truth! (1 Esdras 4:36-40)

And the Lord said to her, **"Speak Truth only, for Truth is of Itself which is God. They may not honor you, but they will honor the Truth you speak."**

On June 4, 1993, Mary Kathryn was in a busy, noisy, airport, awaiting the arrival of a friend. She carried her prayer journal with her everywhere. She took it out and wrote: *"Oh, how I wish I were in a quiet place just now! I have such a longing for my 'quiet time.'"*

Our Lady said to her, **"What would you ask, my child, in your 'quiet time'?"**

(As soon as Our Lady began to speak, all the noise around her disappeared.)

"Father said that he thought the Medal should somehow be linked with the term Miraculous Medal. I would ask what do You think of this, my Lady?"

"It is a term that man understands. If man understood my Immaculate Conception, by which I was created Full of Grace, he would have confidence in that which God created, but instead his focus is on an outward sign created by man which is, as you say, 'linked' with the miraculous.

"As this is so, the outward sign will again be a focus of man's attention as a symbol of God's merciful-power, and man will speak of it in terms he understands. The term does not change the truth of it.

"I am the Immaculate Conception. I am Full of Grace. In me there is no obstacle to God's Grace. I am therefore, a clear channel through which His merciful-power can be transformed, comminuted."

("The term does not change the truth of it." — Mary Kathryn's Spiritual Director decided in the end that the Medal should be called the *Virgin of the Globe,* because that was the title this phase of the Apparitions was given in the beginning. It was the only one to be given two titles — it was also called *The Virgin Most Powerful.* He also decided that the date on the Medal should appear as 1994 instead of 1830, because it was produced in 1994.)

Just then the noise came back, and the plane for which she was waiting arrived, but Mary Kathryn felt somehow that what Our Lady had said was unfinished.

The next day, she read it again, and she looked up the word "comminuted," because she had never heard it before and had no idea what it meant.

Comminute: 1) to pulverize; triturate, 2) Comminuted; divided into small parts, 3) powdered; pulverized.

Triturate: to reduce to fine particles or powder.

(Of course! If God's Merciful-Power were to reach each man in its full strength, so to speak, who could survive it?)

When Mary Kathryn had this more complete understanding, Our Lady continued, **"The outward sign is a symbol of what lies within the heart — of confidence and trust. It is a visible means of communicating this to others and thereby propagating that which lies within, that might otherwise remain hidden.**

"The Two Hearts worn about the neck, close to the heart, is a symbol of the unity thereof.

"Man asks for signs. God also asks for signs. This sign is a token of the heart and the unity of the hearts is miracle working.

"I am the 'link' God has chosen.

"Man asks for gifts and graces and God offers freely to those who love Him; man must do the same for the unity of the hearts to be complete.

"I am Mediatrix. I offer to man what comes from the Heart

of God and to God what comes from the heart of man.

"God has poured out His graces upon the whole world. It is essential now, that those who have received, return what is required for the whole world. Each must offer from his own heart."

When Mary Kathryn shared this with her Spiritual Director, he said, "You had no way of knowing," (it was not common knowledge at that time) "but the Holy Father wants to declare the fifth Marian Dogma." He said that there were three definitions included in this dogma, that of Mary, Coredemptrix, Mediatrix, and Advocate for the people of God. And he told her that the first Medal, the Medal of the Immaculate Conception, preceded the dogma of the Immaculate Conception, and that it helped to promulgate the Dogma. This Medal, he said, shows all three attitudes. Whereas, the first medal showed *only two*. He believed that it, too, could help to promulgate this Final Marian Dogma. Mary Kathryn had no prior knowledge of these things. This quickly became the focus of the Medal, in discussion, print and in presentation.

In her heart, however, Mary Kathryn felt that people would not fully understand without *the rest of the story*. But it seemed that that was not the time for it to be told, except to her Spiritual Director, who did not see the need for it at that time. If Heaven wanted it, the time would come, she thought. And so it has. With her Spiritual Director's permission, it is being presented to you here. *Now,* it appears, there is a "need!"

July 10, 1993, feeling a great hunger for something, though she did not know for what, she said to St. Catherine, "*St. Catherine, please teach me something.*"

With that she opened the book, *Saint Catherine Labouré of the Miraculous Medal,* and this was her prayer journal entry of that date:

> …These last years are an excellent source for the student of her sanctity. Her secret lay in the fact that she did what she was supposed to do, as well as she could, and for God. It was as simple as that. There can be no doubt that she did not do a particular work as well at sixty-eight as she had done at twenty-eight. *She did it*

as well as she could—that was the point — and it was just as pleasing to God, for her heart and soul were in it, and He was both. God is the only master Who rewards effort rather than result.

*"Yes, I will do as well as I can for as long as God chooses for me to remain on this earth. Thank you for this example, dear St. Catherine, **dear** friend."*

Then she turned to and wrote down the account of what St. Catherine revealed to her superior the year before her death, and her insistence that the statue be made.

After that her exhaustion was so great, she felt she had to go to bed, but she was not allowed to sleep. She felt compelled to get up and *finish* reading the book, *Saint Catherine Laboure of the Miraculous Medal,* which she had not done up to that time.

"At last! I've finished the book!"

And St. Catherine said to her, **"And so you have the final command."**

"The statue!"

"Yes, it 'too' must be 'completed.' I did what I was suppose to do as well as I could. Now you must do the same. You must bring to completion that for which She asked. She who is the Immaculate Conception."

"What did happen to the ball? Can you tell me?"

"The time will come again when the world will cry, 'O Mary conceived without sin, pray for us who have recourse to thee.' It will be the battle cry of Her army, of those consecrated to Her Immaculate Heart, the Knights of the Immaculata.

"When this happens, the voices of these consecrated souls shall be raised to heaven in unison and the time of Justice shall overlap the time of Mercy. Then shall be the time of fullness. Then shall Her role as Mediatrix culminate. Were She not the Mother of Mercy, Justice alone would prevail.

"Had the world responded to Her call these many times, there would be no reason to fear Justice at all."

Mary Kathryn said, *"Our Lady said 'Now is the time of fullness.'"*

"And so it is," said St. Catherine. "Hence, the need for the completion of the medal at this time.

"Think of the moon as the lantern of Mercy and the time has begun for the eclipse by the Sun of Justice. It has indeed begun, but is not yet full. There is still time for many to prepare for the darkness.

"Great shall be the protection of those who wear this medal about their neck, and recite, with confidence, the words of the prayer: 'O Mary, conceived without sin, pray for us who have recourse to thee.'

"And great shall be the battle between Her children and the children of the serpent.

"The ball, which is the symbol of Her intercession, in offering to God what comes from the heart of man, can only be returned to Her hands by the offering of that which is required for the whole world, but each must offer from his own heart, and the power of the whole will be constituted by the sum of the prayers and sacrifices of each individual.

"The out-pouring of graces is ever-present for those who ask. However, *had I not insisted on the statue, only half of the story would have been told* — even now, the world must be reminded, 'unto whom much is given, much will be required'."

"To be complete, the two must be as one. Now is the time of fullness."

"Thank you. I will do as well as I can. Please pray for me."

Culminate: to rise to or form an apex (summit) — to *complete*. *(Random House Dictionary of the English Language)*

July 20, 1993, during Holy Mass on EWTN, Mary Kathryn heard these words in the homily and entered them into her prayer journal: "...See within the present moment the hand of God.... Follow with the blind trust of a little child. Let Him take us where He wants us...."

"Lord God, help me to desire only and always your holy will."

"...So we ask Our Holy Mother, help us to always seek, desire and follow the holy will of God.... Let that be our home, the holy will of God."

"Amen," she wrote.

(Those words would have great meaning to her in the near future. She would not be able to continue working, and would have to give up her home, the chapel and the Rosary Garden she loved so dearly.)

Later that afternoon she saw internally three pictures: first, the one a young boy had tried to draw of the Virgin of the Globe, but he could not draw Her arms and hands holding the golden ball, though he tried. The second was only her forearms extended out from flowing sleeves, and She was holding the golden ball — nothing more. And the third, was the completed picture of the Virgin of the Globe. These three pictures told the story: *"We must have confidence in God and in Your intercession, (Blessed Mother), and we must offer prayers and sacrifices from our own hearts . . . — This is what the golden ball represents — **our part!** — the whole world, and each individual!"*

On July 22, 1993 she was led to this Scripture: "Happy are those whose greatest desire is to do what God requires; God will satisfy them fully!" (Matthew 5:6)

And then,

> Of course, nobody who has been drinking old wine will want the new at once. He is sure to say, "The old is good sound wine." In short, Jesus tells us plainly that He does not even expect people to like His new venture; it is altogether too novel and therefore uncomfortable.... Will people resist us? Yes, says Christ, they will, and this is exactly what we ought to expect. People simply do not like new wine, it is too disturbing to their peace of mind. They like things that are orderly and therefore calculable ... we have Christ's word for it that there will be resistance. The teaching of Christ does not lead us to expectations of easy success or easy lives. It teaches us rather, to be realistic about human nature....
>
> Christ had to wage a battle because the things for which He stood were intrinsically threatening to those in power, either politically or religiously. The fierce-

ness of the struggle made choice necessary and with choice came inevitable division among men. The people who wanted to smooth things over and to be friends with everybody, thus avoiding all tension, were simply naïve, for life is not ordered that way. Herein lies the tremendous import of Christ's words, "Do not think that I have come to bring peace on earth; I have not come to bring peace, but a sword." (Matthew 10:34) Luke amplifies the saying by adding, "No I tell you, but rather division." (Luke 12:51)

...Though only his enemies call Him a drunkard, it is obvious that Christ drank wine. It was His general reputation for gaiety which provided the basis for one of His most humorous rejoinders, to the effect that the critics could not be pleased. If people didn't like the abstemiousness of John, and if they also did not like the gaiety of Jesus, what did they want?

To what then shall I compare the men of this generation, and what are they like? They are like children sitting in the market place and calling one another, "We piped to you, and you did not dance; we wailed, and you did not weep! For John the Baptist has come eating no bread and drinking no wine; and you say, "He has a demon." The Son of Man has come eating and drinking; and you say, "Behold, a glutton and a drunkard, a friend of tax collectors and sinners! Yet wisdom is justified by all her children." (Luke 7:31-35)

The sharp thrust of this final line is characteristic of Christ's sly humor. He is willing to rest the case in terms of human consequences. What happens in the lives of men and women is the real test of His position or any other. His bad reputation among the pious is a trivial matter, provided the lives of ordinary people are enriched and glorified. "I'll judge by My consequences, if you will judge by yours" He is saying in a most pithy manner. *(The Humor of Christ)*

Then the Lord asked, **"Do you see the humor in this, my child?"**

"Not really, Lord," she said. *"I see lessons, but I miss the humor."*

He said to her, **"At Cana, My Mother said, 'Do whatever He tells you,' and it was done, as required, for the making of new wine. And it was expected, even then, that the new wine would not equal the old, yet when it was tasted it was found superior for I had made it so.**

"Taste and see the goodness of the Lord, and others will follow, but not all. And some more slowly than others, but all who drink thereof shall be fully satisfied.

"Who then shall have chosen the better? And who smiled?"

"Those who chose the new wine chose the better. And Your Mother smiled."

Then Our Lady said, **"Do whatever He tells you, and see the consequences thereof."**

"Yes, Blessed Mother."

"Your business is to follow Me." (John 21:22)

In August and September, Mary Kathryn's strength decreased rapidly and dramatically, to the point that she had to force herself even to walk from room to room or to eat a few bites of food, as she knew she must do to maintain any strength at all. Her last day of work was September 30th. She left with the blessings and prayers of this kind doctor. There was nothing left but to completely abandon herself to the Good God.

October 1st was the Feast of St. Terese of the Child Jesus and the Holy Face. So she prayed to her: *"O dear St. Therese, help me in all that is, and all that is to come. Teach me, ever more deeply, your 'little way.' I love you."*

And the Lord began to teach her more deeply the Joy of Suffering. He led her, for the first time, to *The Story of a Soul* and to *John of the Cross for Today*. And so, she said, it seemed to her that she was walking down a path with these two friends, discussing their spiritual journeys and shedding light on hers.

October 28, 1993, from *The Story of a Soul* she read and entered into her prayer journal: "I opened the Epistles of St. Paul. My eyes lighted on Chapter XII and XIII of his First Epistle to the Corinthians, where he says we cannot all be apostles, prophets and doctors, that the Church is made up of a number of different members and that the eye cannot also be the hand."

And Mary Kathryn pictured herself as a thumbnail, thinking to herself, *"Sometimes there is a little job for which even that little thumbnail is very useful, though most of the time it is just there."* She smiled to herself and said, *"How wonderful that is. In His Mercy, He allows it to be that way!"*

And Our Lady said, **"In His Wisdom, my child."**

For many years, Mary Kathryn had been taught by God through many gifts and graces, by His design and for His purpose. Now she would learn, as well, from His withdrawal.

On October 31, 1993, All Hallows Eve, Mary Kathryn offered herself as a "Victim to His Merciful-Love," as "little Therese" had done.

She had been told to pray for the Americas, **"In a special way"** — she did not know what that "special way" was, but she was told that the Lord would lead her to it.

Later, she was given the opportunity to ask one thing of the Child Jesus (the Infant of Prague), Whom she loved dearly, and so, in this she saw the opportunity to pray in that "special way."

"...I pray for the Americas. I ask for Conversion and Mercy. I ask it in Your Holy Name, Sweet Jesus."

And the Lord said to her, **"You who have a child's heart have asked with great wisdom and great faith."**

"Jesus, I trust in You.

"And now dear Lord, speaking about a child's heart." And she prayed for things concerning her children. *"...This I ask from a mother's heart for her children."*

The Lord said, **"The mother's heart asks believing that God can. The child's heart asks believing that God will."**

She understood by this that her faith was not as strong in her prayer for her children as it was in her prayer for the Americas. So she said to Him, *"Then increase my faith, Lord."*

Quick as that, she was plunged into the Dark Night of the Spirit, which is a painful and total walk in pure Faith. This would last for fifteen months.

(For those of you who do not know what the Dark Night of the Spirit is, refer to the writings of St. John of the Cross.)

During most of this time, by God's design, she lived in the back of an old Mission. *"God was hidden from me. I could no longer feel His Presence, but I knew where He was — in the Tabernacle — and He had placed me, right next door."*

It was during this time, on September 17, 1994, that the Virgin of the Globe Medal was introduced to the public by Mary Kathryn's Spiritual Director.

It was produced by Creed, and since then tens of thousands have been circulated. However, not all were accompanied by the written explanation (as had been planned), which was, at that time, limited to the connection between the Medal and the fifth Marian Dogma. It lacked *the rest of the story,* which is told here.

It is being provided at this time, believing this to be *God's time!*

It was also during this time that Mary Kathryn took private perpetual vows on November 1, 1995 with the permission of her Spiritual Director.

Later, she would embrace Carmelite spirituality, and she would dedicate her life to God in the service of the Church, living the "little way," while at the same time, fulfilling her other vocations as mother and grandmother — just as her mother had said so many years before.

She has lived a very hidden life which she says is *"A great blessing from God. It is not my medal, it is St.Catherine's 'Other Medal,' requested of her by Our Lady. And as St. Catherine said, '...* **The Divine Plan is His (God's).... We are all but servants....** *'*

"The first medal did not portray the uplifted golden ball; the first statue of the Virgin of the Globe had no rays streaming from the rings on Our Lady's fingers. The Blessed Mother said, **'To be complete, the two must be as one.'** *And Catherine told me I would see the completion of her mission. The first 'complete' statue was finished January 6, 2001*

*"I believe with my whole heart that the people really need to know **the rest of the story** in order to truly understand, and they need to know it **now!***

"With the First Medal, the Medal of the Immaculate Concep-tion, Our Lady promised a great outpouring of graces, and the world has seen just that. That is why the people named that medal the Miraculous Medal — a term they understood.

"She said the people will come, as well, to speak of this Medal, the Virgin of the Globe/The Virgin Most Powerful, **'in terms they understand....'**

"But most importantly, She promised that those who will wear it around their neck, pray the little prayer, and have confidence in God and in Her intercession, will receive **'great protection in these days of battle!'"**

Our hope is three-fold: 1) To propagate the Medal *with full understanding of it.* 2) To urge the people of God to do *their part,* (the golden ball), — to offer up their prayers and sacrifices *for the whole world,* and 3) To promulgate the fifth and final Marian Dogma: *Mary, Coredemptrix, Mediatrix, and Advocate for the people of God.* All three roles are portrayed, in fullness, on The Medal of the Virgin of the Globe/The Virgin Most Powerful.

Heaven knew the time would come for this "phase" of the Medal, and **the time is now!**

Novena to the Virgin of the Globe

O Mary, conceived without sin, **Co-redemptrix** —willing
participant in Jesus' great work of salvation, teach us to
work with Him for the salvation of our neighbor.
Pray for us who have recourse to Thee!

(here make the sign of the cross)

O Mary, conceived without sin, **Mediatrix** of all graces and
Mother of every soul, let the graces we receive through your
hands be met with profound gratitude and sincere cooperation.
Pray for us who have recourse to Thee!

(here make the sign of the cross)

O Mary, conceived without sin, **Advocate** for the people of
God, from the moment of the Annunciation until the end of
time, lift up our deeply wounded world to God's merciful love.
Pray for us who have recourse to Thee!

(here make the sign of the cross)

(State your request/intention)

Our Father
Hail Mary
Glory be

(here make the sign of the cross and say)

Father, Thy Will be done! Amen